Chinese Cut-Paper
Animal Designs

Dover Publications, Inc.
Mineola, New York

The publisher is grateful to Florence Temko for making available the contents of her personal Chinese cut-paper collection as well as examples from her book, *Chinese Paper Cuts: Their History, How to Use Them, How to Make Them,* San Francisco: China Books, 1982, for our publication.

Copyright

Bibliographical Note

Chinese Cut-Paper Animal Designs is a new work, first published by Dover Publications, Inc., in 2006.

DOVER *Pictorial Archive* SERIES

Library of Congress Cataloging-in-Publication Data

Chinese cut-paper animal designs.
    p. cm.—(Dover pictorial archive series)
    ISBN 0-486-45225-5 (pbk.)
    1. Paper work—China. 2. Decoration and ornament—Animal forms—China.

NK8553.2.C6C436 2006
736'.980951—dc22
                                    2006048598

Manufactured in the United States of America
Dover Publications, Inc., 31 East 2nd Street, Mineola, N.Y. 11501

16

20

27

39

47

50